Jarrold Wild Flowers Se
With text by **E. A. Ellis**

Wild Flowers of the Moors and Heaths

Jarrold Colour Publications, Norwich

1 × 3·0

1. TORMENTIL (*Potentilla erecta*). Distinguished from other small yellow-flowered species of *Potentilla* by its trefoil leaves, this is a common perennial herb of peatlands throughout Britain. The wiry, reddish rootstocks are crowned by dense rosettes of foliage which die down as flowering stems develop. The flowers appear from June to September and make a brilliant show in sunny situations. Normally they have only four petals, which soon drop. In wet habitats the stems and leaves are often distorted by a yellow parasitic fungus (*Taphrina potentillae*).

Nothing except a view of the sea evokes such a sense of freedom as the contemplation of a vast expanse of heath or moorland, with the purple of heather and the vivid green of bog mosses dappling the scene in the play of sunlight and moving cloud shadows. It is this overall beauty, reflecting every mood of Nature, which casts a spell on those who visit the Scottish Highlands, the hills and dales of Yorkshire and Westmorland, Ireland's mossy, lake-strewn wastes, or the wild regions of Exmoor and Dartmoor. Instinctively, one is aware of a special relationship between the plant life of such bleak, windswept and often rain- and mist-drenched country and the raw impact of the physical environment. In places the vegetation barely covers the rocks and infertile sands. Pioneering algae, lichens and mosses are much in evidence as primary colonists of open ground, where they form the first faint traces of peat, as they do on Arctic wastes. In the wettest places, bog mosses (*Sphagnum*) blanket great expanses of land, holding rainwater like a sponge. They form green hummocks on the bogs and provide habitats for certain rushes, sedges, orchids, heathers and other flowering plants. In some areas great thicknesses of peat have been accumulating, mainly from mosses, for three or four thousand years under the influence of a continuously wet climate. Elsewhere, some bogs have developed over drowned forests where the remains of ancient trees can still be found preserved in the sterile peat.

Most of Britain's true moorland stands at more than 800 ft above sea-level, in the west and north-west, where the rainfall averages 50 in. or more in the year. The higher one goes, the later plants of the same kind come into bloom. The rock-beds of moors are generally devoid of lime, so the ground-water and peat remain in an acid condition. The peat also tends to lack oxygen; earthworms cannot live in it and it cannot support aerobic bacteria which are able to convert dead vegetable matter into fertile soil and at the same time produce the nitrates which plants require for healthy growth. This work is carried out chiefly by subterranean fungi which are able to thrive in the airless, acid environment, and these fungi often grow in close association with the roots of bog and heath plants which are dependent on them for survival. Insectivorous plants such as the sundews and butterworts obtain their nitrogen from living prey caught on their sticky leaves. There is often a lot of iron in bog water and some plants are able to use this for their growth chemistry in place of lime. Sometimes, springs or streams bring flushes of richer and perhaps limy soil into bogs, greatly encouraging the increase of certain plants. The dominant plant cover varies from practically pure bog-moss in the wettest parts to pure ling-heather in the driest, with a whole range of mixtures between.

In some areas bog-cotton brightens the darkling scene in summer, or the golden stars of asphodel rim the hollows. Tufts of deer-sedge and purple moor-grass, rosy bog-heather (Cross-leaved Heath) or straggling bushes of bilberry may be the most noticeable features, according to local circumstances of climate, drainage or land-use. The management of moorland over the centuries has brought changes. There are vast areas now too well drained for the bog-mosses to survive where they flourished in the past and built up most of the existing peat. Grazing by red deer and sheep can have a powerful selective effect on the plant life and result in the spread of grass turf at the expense of more tender vegetation. Heather is often burnt to encourage the growth of young shoots for sheep and grouse, while the ash provides mineral enrichment for the topsoil. Some large tracts of bog have been deeply drained for the extraction of peat-moss on a commercial scale in recent years and this has resulted in the loss of interesting plant communities. When peat is dried and exposed to the air it shrinks and becomes oxidised. In this condition it may be blown away as dust very easily and it is eroded very swiftly when streams sweep down from the hills in spate during the winter.

Our lowland heaths have developed on poor, acid and mainly sandy soils which were once forest land. Following tree-clearance, their rich topsoil was soon lost and where heather, bracken and gorse now thrive, one finds only a thin layer of peat at the surface. Beneath this lies a zone of peat-stained sand, then silver-sand and, finally, a seam of black humus trapped by a lower 'pan' of iron-bound sand or gravel which arrests the seepage of water. This 'podsol' structure, as it is called, is characteristic of English heaths, some of which are on the ancient Greensand and others on glacial sands. The heaths of East Anglia's Breckland were once mainly sheep-walks and they have developed on thin, lime-leached soils in this area of low rainfall. Some patches of damp heathland have developed in the hollows ('slacks') of old sand dunes.

Heath fires are all too frequent and can be very damaging to both plant and animal life, but some vegetation is able to recover fairly quickly. Gorse and heather sprout again from burnt stubs and their seedlings come up from the bare patches, while spores of bracken are often quick to colonise scorched ground along with the mosses and lichens that flourish wherever the soil surface has been sterilised by fire. Unfortunately, while some species are able to regenerate, others are more sensitive and tend to be ousted; so the overall diversity of the vegetation is reduced. On moorlands, with their severe climate, poor drainage and widespread grazing by sheep, invasion by trees is discouraged. So the open landscape persists, with its drifts of blossom and sparkling verdure in summer, the russet and gold of dying vegetation in autumn and the austere majesty of a primeval world settling upon it in winter. The animal life of this bleak countryside is exposed to great climatic extremes; but bog pools harbour special dragonflies and water-beetles; the heather sustains the caterpillars of a great variety of moths and is the habitat of peculiar plant bugs and spiders. Lizards and adders abound. Curlew and golden plover bring wild music to the moors in spring, and skylarks are universal in the summer scene, while red grouse are at home in the heather throughout the year. The southern heaths also have their special birds, reptiles and sun-loving insects. In the lowlands there is a tendency for the trees of acid soils, such as birch, pine and oak to colonise all but the wettest ground in the course of time; but frequent heathfires usually prevent this, while in other respects they only bring disaster upon a wonderland of varied wildlife. We can expect the area now covered by heath and moorland in this country to be greatly encroached upon in the fairly near future; but our native love of freedom is perhaps the surest guarantee that a goodly sample will survive for ages to come.

The lowland heaths of England are most dangerously threatened, not only by the encroachments of agriculture, forestry, housing and holiday development, but often by over-drainage undertaken for the benefit of the surrounding countryside. We have to look increasingly to the efforts made by county naturalists' trusts in conserving the best of these heaths, and it is more than ever necessary that those who visit these attractive areas for pleasure should have special regard to fire risks. Scotland's wealth of wild moors might be thought immune from the prospect of material change, but with enhanced resources of power from offshore oil and gas, increasing industrialisation is bound to follow, bringinging conservation problems for many a beauty spot in the Highlands.

Figures in red beside each picture show the scale of reproduction

2 × 0·5
3 × 1·0

2. BELL HEATHER (*Erica cinerea*). This deep purple heather, a strictly west European species widespread in Britain, flourishes on the drier parts of heaths and moors, avoiding all but the most acid soils. The flowers are usually at their best in August and are much visited by bumble-bees and certain butterflies. In the heat of the day they produce a characteristic honey scent. Plants with pure white flowers can be found occasionally, also pale purple varieties.

3. EYEBRIGHT (*Euphrasia pseudo-kerneri*). The eyebrights are rather dwarf, wiry annuals belonging to the figwort family. Numerous species grow in grassy and heathy places, several being restricted to the coast, especially in the north and west of Britain. They show much variation and are often difficult to identify. The large-flowered species illustrated is found mainly in south-east England, often on limestone grassland and sometimes in fens. All are partial parasites of grass roots.

4. LING (*Calluna vulgaris*). Our commonest heather, flourishing on acid peat and sand in both lowland and upland districts. It forms large bushy hummocks which have an active life of about twenty-five years. Periodic burning stimulates new growth which provides good grazing for sheep and grouse. Besoms used to be made from the springy twigs. The crowded pearly flowers contain much nectar and attract many kinds of bees and flies, mainly in August and September.

5. HAREBELL (*Campanula rotundifolia*). This slender perennial, the 'bluebell' of Scotland, grows commonly in dry, acid grassland and sandy soils almost throughout Britain. The basal leaves are rounded and those on the flower-stalks narrow and almost grass-like. The delicate flowers, which are scentless, appear from July to September and are visited by butterflies and bees, including the very small Harebell Carpenter Bee which shows a preference for their pollen and nectar.

4 × 0·5
5 × 1·0

6. DODDER (*Cuscuta epithymum*). Dodders could be called the vampires of the plant world, since they feed wholly on the sap of other species. They are members of the bindweed family which have adopted a parasitic habit. Seeds germinating on the ground in May put forth fine threads which coil round wild thyme, heather and gorse and develop suckers which absorb nourishment from the stems. During the summer their nest-like webs of red threads smother the host-plants and bear clusters of sweetly scented flowers from July to September.

7. DORSET HEATH (*Erica ciliaris*). This graceful heather inhabits the extreme west of Europe bordering the Atlantic. In Britain it is confined to a few damp, sandy heaths in Dorset, Devon and Cornwall. It grows to a height of 2½ ft. The stems are downy and the leaves, which are fringed with fine hairs, usually grow in whorls of three. The long, tubular flowers mature from June to September and have dark, narrow mouths with pin-like styles protruding. In Dorset this species sometimes hybridises with the Cross-leaved Heath.

6 × 8·0

8 × 1·5

8. CROSS-LEAVED HEATH (*Erica tetralix*). A characteristic plant of wet heaths and bogs, with downy, grey-green foliage and leaves arranged in whorls of four. The flowers are usually flushed with rose, or may be white; they have narrow mouths and are commonly self-fertilised, though they can be pollinated by very small insects. Confined to western Europe, this species ranges from Norway down to Portugal. Blooming from June to September, it survives burning and partial shading by trees and bushes. It has been used like hops for brewing beer.

9. ST DABEOC'S HEATH (*Dabeocia cantabrica*). A native of rocky heaths in western Ireland (West Galway and Mayo), this shrubby plant is naturalised here and there in England and Scotland. It thrives where the climate is wet and there is little frost in winter. Growing in scattered clumps, it blooms freely from June to September in open situations, but not in the shade. The flowers are visited by several kinds of bumble-bees. Nowadays found chiefly in Spain, it may have survived the last Ice Age on Ireland's Atlantic coast.

10. PETTY WHIN (*Genista anglica*). Also known as Needle Whin, this little shrub attains a height of only about 2 ft and has very slender, smooth branches armed with long, slightly curved spines. It is widely distributed on heaths and moors, though absent from Ireland, and tends to grow in fairly dry places. The shining yellow blossoms appear chiefly in May and June and are succeeded by smooth, inflated pods. The flowers are attractive to bees, but yield only pollen. Many of the seeds are destroyed by small weevils.

11. WESTERN DWARF GORSE (*Ulex gallii*). This strongly prickly autumn-flowering shrub flourishes on acid, often grassy, heaths mainly in the west of England and Wales and in southern Ireland, although it is to be found here and there outside these regions. The bushes are sturdy and usually dark green and the flowers are typically of a rich golden colour, with standards more than 12·0 mm long and boldly curved wings projecting beyond the keel, while the silky calyx is over 9·5 mm long. The pods scatter seeds violently in spring.

10 × 2·0
11 × 0·5

12. SOUTHERN DWARF GORSE (*Ulex minor*). This abounds on old heathlands in south-east England, but is absent from the north and west of Britain and from the whole of Ireland. It is generally smaller and less fiercely prickly than *Ulex gallii*, with downy, usually light green and often prostrate branches. The spines are dense, but relatively weak. The flowers (August to September) are typically lemon coloured, with standards less than 12·0 mm long and wings only slightly curved and seldom projecting beyond the keel. The calyx is less than 9·5 mm long, with a sparse coating of adpressed silky hairs. This species can hybridise with the Western Dwarf Gorse.

13. COMMON GORSE (*Ulex europaeus*). Also known as furze or whin, this prickly west European shrub thrives mainly on poor, acid soils and makes a glorious show of yellow blossoms on many of our heaths and commons in spring. Some of the bushes can be found in bloom at all seasons. After heath fires, gorse soon sprouts again from the charred stumps and in the following spring great numbers of seedlings come up, since the seeds are very resistant to heat. In the past, bushes were cut for fuel by the poor and used as thatch for cottages and farm buildings, also for fencing and to protect crops from grazing animals.

14. BROOM (*Sarothamnus scoparius*). A brushy shrub with slender, five-angled green twigs and a few trefoil leaves. The twigs do much of the work normally carried out by leaves. This species is common in dry, sandy places, avoiding all traces of lime in the soil. The main flowering time is in May and June; the blossoms have no nectar but are visited by bees for pollen. The twigs were formerly used in basket-work and made into besoms. They can be steeped in hot water to produce a hair-wash, and a heart medicine is obtained from them. Wine is made from the flowers, but the leaves are poisonous.

12 × 0·5
13 × 0·25

14 × 0·2

15 × 1·0

16 × 1·0

17 × 1·0

15. WOOD SAGE (*Teucrium scorodonia*). A perennial herb common on well-drained and usually acid soils throughout Britain, especially on heaths and often in the partial shade of trees. It has woody stems and crinkled, softly downy leaves which emit a strong odour like a mixture of garden sage and garlic when bruised. They are often deformed by a rust fungus (*Puccinia annularis*). The flowers are great favourites with bees from July to September.

16. WHITE CLIMBING FUMITORY (*Corydalis claviculata*). A slender and delicate climbing annual with forked tendrils extending from the tips of its compound and rather fern-like leaves. It is widespread in England, Wales and Scotland, but rare in Ireland, having a patchy distribution though it can be plentiful on light acid soils in the partial shade of trees, bracken or rocks. The flowers develop from June to September in long-stalked clusters directly opposite the leaves.

17. WILD THYME (*Thymus pulegioides*). Three kinds of thyme grow wild in Britain, all of them frequenting dry, grassy or heathy situations. *T. pulegioides*, commonest in south-east England, is larger and more aromatic than the others. It grows in tufts, often on ant-hills. The stems are square, with sharply defined keels and the leaves are smooth. The flowers open from July to September and are attractive to bees and butterflies. The terminal leaves are often affected by gall-mites.

18. ACRID LOBELIA (*Lobelia urens*). A rare perennial herb found on a few acid heaths in southern England. A rosette of leaves develops in spring and the flowers appear from July to September, being visited by flies, 'skipper' butterflies and day-flying moths. The seedlings need plenty of light and colonies flourish best when tall competing vegetation is cleared by fire or grazing animals. This plant has an acrid, milky juice which can produce blisters, as a defence against grazing animals.

18 × 2·0

19. SELF-HEAL (*Prunella vulgaris*). A very common low-growing perennial of open, turfy habitats, including parts of heathy commons where the soil is least acid. In very dry places it may be dwarfed and yet manage to flower profusely all through the summer. The flowers are usually violet coloured, but may be pink or white; they vary much in size on different plants, some being small and wholly female. Known also as hook-heal, sicklewort and Carpenter's Herb, this plant has an ancient reputation for healing wounds quickly.

20. MAIDEN PINK (*Dianthus deltoides*). This narrow-leaved perennial can be found here and there on heath grasslands and hill pastures, but has vanished from many of its former haunts in recent years. The pink or white speckled flowers develop singly or in twos and threes and are not fragrant like most of its relatives; all the same, they attract butterflies and moths by day. They are in bloom from June to September, opening only in sunshine. Varieties of this species are cultivated in rock gardens.

21. MOSSY TILLAEA (*Crassula tillaea*). This diminutive annual plant is virtually confined to East Anglia, the south of England and the Channel Islands. It forms carpets on sandy and gravelly heathlands, mainly on well-trodden paths which hold moisture, and in areas closely nibbled by rabbits. Although often greenish when young, or in shade, it usually develops a vivid scarlet colour which makes it very conspicuous. The minute white flowers come in June and July, but are hidden by the pointed sepals which surround them.

19 × 2·0

20 × 1·0

21 × 1·0

22 × 2·0

22. MOUNTAIN PANSY (*Viola lutea*). This showiest of our wild pansies attains a height of about 4 in. and persists from year to year by means of creeping underground shoots. It flourishes on grassy, slightly acid soils derived from limestone rocks on mountains in the north of Britain The flowers are commonly bright yellow, but may be suffused with violet or lavender; they measure 1¼ in. vertically and have short, slender spurs. The lower leaves are long-stalked and rather narrow. Flowering continues from spring to late summer.

23 × 3·0
24 × 0·5

25 × 0·3

23. LESSER SPEARWORT (*Ranunculus flammula*). A small-flowered buttercup with smooth, narrow, often grass-like leaves, common in wet, peaty places throughout the British Isles. It produces a succession of blossoms from May to September and the fruits are in small globular heads. Although highly poisonous to livestock, it is usually avoided by grazing beasts on account of its very acrid taste. A dwarf, matted form grows on exposed sea coasts in the north. The plants vary greatly in size.

24. HARE'S-TAIL (*Eriophorum vaginatum*). This bristle-leaved, tussocky cotton-sedge flourishes in moorland bogs, chiefly in areas of high rainfall in the north, where it grows even on mountain summits. The solitary, stiffly erect and almost spherical flower-spikes appear in May and June; they are at first black, with a silvery sheen, but soon become white and fluffy. The grubs of a beautiful metallic beetle (*Plateumaris discolor*) feed on the roots, tapping air supplies from the plant's tissues.

25. COTTON-GRASS (*Eriophorum angustifolium*). A narrow-leaved bog-cotton found in boggy places throughout Britain, except where drainage has eliminated it from some of its old haunts. The dark-brown flower-spikes form umbel-like, slightly drooping sprays at the tips of wiry stalks. In summer these become snowy with silken fluff which has in the past been collected for stuffing mattresses, cushions and pillows and making lamp wicks.

26. BOG ASPHODEL (*Narthecium ossifragum*). From July to September the great mossy bogs of Scotland, Ireland, Wales and western England are starry with the gleaming blossoms of this plant. As autumn approaches, orange-coloured capsules ripen and the stems turn red. It used to be said that bog asphodel was the cause of sheep-rot (*ossifragum* means 'bone-breaker'), but this has been proved untrue. The seeds have forked beaks which help them to float and reach new ground in times of flood.

26 × 1·0

27 × 1·5

28 × 1·5
29 × 1·0

27. RED RATTLE (*Pedicularis palustris*). A common annual herb of wet heaths and peaty fens. The spikes of purplish-pink, hooded blossoms may stand 2 ft high. As the flowers wither, their calices swell and become bladder-like, and when the seeds ripen, they rattle when the papery holders are shaken. Though resembling Heath Lousewort, it differs in having hairs on the calyx and four (not two) teeth on the upper lip of the corolla.

28. YELLOW RATTLE (*Rhinanthus minor*). This is one of several rather similar species which are half-parasitic, taking some nourishment from grass roots, but also manufacturing food with the help of their own leaves. It grows in a variety of grassy habitats and blooms in early summer. The seeds are flattened and ear-shaped and rattle inside their capsules when shaken by the wind; they have winged margins which help air-dispersal; they also float readily when the ground is flooded.

29. MARSH GENTIAN (*Gentiana pneumonanthe*). A rather rare perennial of damp lowland heaths, growing mainly where the subsoil is sandy. The plants vary much in size, the tallest spikes reaching a height of 18 in. and bearing up to twenty-eight blossoms. The flowers are found from July to September and are usually dark blue, with green stripes, but may be pink or white occasionally. They are visited chiefly by bumble-bees and pollen-beetles. The seeds are also by Tortricid caterpillars.

30. MILKWORT (*Polygala vulgaris*). Two kinds of milkwort are common and widely distributed on our heathlands. Both are small, loosely sprawling plants with rather narrow, pointed leaves, prettily veined sepals and bright blue, purple, pink or white flowers. *P. vulgaris* has its stem leaves arranged alternately at wide intervals and the flower spikes are long; *P. serpyllifolia* has at least the lower stem leaves in opposite pairs, while the flower heads are shorter; it is commonest on acid soils.

31 × 1·5

32 × 1·0

33 × 1·0

31. ROUND-LEAVED WINTERGREEN (*Pyrola rotundifolia*). The wintergreens are all smooth-leaved evergreen herbs with creeping rootstocks. This species is rare and very localised, though it has a wide range in Britain. It inhabits fens, bogs and the acid, peaty hollows of sand dunes. In shady places it produces only quantities of glossy foliage, but in more open spots its elegant blossoms, appearing rather like Lilies of the Valley, though usually tinged with pink, may be found from July to September; they are sweetly scented.

32. BOG PIMPERNEL (*Anagallis tenella*). A creeping plant often very plentiful round the edges of bog pools and found mixed with lush mosses in wet turf. Where the habitat is exposed to plenty of sunlight, but does not dry out, vast numbers of the delicate pink blossoms form shining carpets in summer. It often thrives where land-springs produce 'flushes' in peat-filled valleys. Though among the first species to disappear when fens and bogs are drained it can also be an early colonist of newly flooded peatland.

33. BOG ORCHID (*Hammarbya paludosa*). This smallest of our orchids, sometimes no more than an inch tall, is restricted to bog pools where its yellow-green colour makes it difficult to notice on cushions of bog-moss. Its flowers differ from other orchids in having a lip at the top instead of below. It stores food in a bulb-like stem base and young plants develop from buds on the edges of the small, spoon-like leaves. Most of its nourishment is obtained from a fungus attached to the roots.

34. MARSH ANDROMEDA (*Andromeda polifolia*). This attractive member of the heather family can be found growing in a straggly fashion here and there on the great peat-mosses of north-west England, Wales and Ireland, but only where wet 'blanket bog' conditions prevail. It is an early casualty when bogs are drained and excavated for peat. It grows to a height of about 1 ft and the leaves are greyish green above and white beneath. The nodding pink or white flowers appear in May and June.

34 × 3·0

35 × 2·0

35. HEATH SPOTTED ORCHID (*Dactylorhiza ericetorum*). This is one of a group of orchids characterised by their spreading, finger-like tubers. It is widespread on wet acid heaths and moors, being specially plentiful in the north and west of Britain. The leaves tend to be narrower and more lightly spotted than those of the spotted orchid common on less acid soils. The flowers vary in colour, but are usually pale lilac with very broad, minutely speckled lips. In various parts of its range it blooms between May and August.

36. LESSER BUTTERFLY ORCHID (*Platanthera bifolia*). Although found typically on wet heaths and moors, this species is not completely restricted to acid soils and can be seen occasionally on chalk downs. It frequents both wet and dry habitats. Widely distributed in these islands, it is commonest in the north. The very fragrant flowers appear in June and July and are attractive mainly to moths and butterflies which can reach the nectar in their long spurs. As in many other orchids, a symbiotic root-fungus helps with nutrition, chiefly by making nitrogen available. The twin leaves are broad and usually dark green and the rather slender spikes may carry up to fifteen creamy or faintly greenish flowers. At the end of the season food is stored in newly formed tubers which produce the next year's flowers.

37. DWARF PURPLE ORCHID (*Dactylorhiza purpurella*). This sturdy little marsh orchid has a distinctly northern distribution in Britain, although its range extends to Wales and Ireland in the west. Though often found in bogs, it seems to need some natural irrigation with water bringing calcium from rocks or shell deposits; it is not at home in the most acid parts of moorland. The leaves spread rather openly and have hooded tips; they are of a rich green colour, usually, but not always, with some small dark spots. The flowers seldom open before late June and are generally bright rosy purple, but may be more faintly rosy or darker and redder. This species hybridises with other marsh orchids and with the spotted, fragrant and frog orchids occasionally.

36 × 0·5

37 × 1·2

38. BLOOD-DROP EMLETS (*Mimulus luteus*). The sides of burns and boggy pools in a good many places in Scotland and northern England are resplendent with these bright yellow, red-blotched trumpet-flowers in late summer nowadays. Introduced from Chile early in the nineteenth century, this glossy-leaved species has run wild mainly in the north, whereas its relative the Monkey-flower (*M. guttatus*), introduced from North America at about the same time, is much more widespread along our riversides. The latter has only a few small red spots in its mainly yellow blossoms and its leaves are downy above.

39. COMMON BUTTERWORT (*Pinguicula vulgaris*). This insectivorous plant gets its common name from the pale yellowish colour of its basal rosettes of leaves. These are covered with little knobbed hairs and sticky glands which trap insects such as gnats and midges. When an insect is caught, the leaf edges curl inwards to enfold it and concentrate a flow of digestive juices round its body. This butterwort is common in bogs, especially in mountainous country; though widely distributed in Britain, it is somewhat rare in the south. It flowers in May and June and over-winters by means of rootless buds which may be dispersed by floods.

40. PALE BUTTERWORT (*Pinguicula lusitanica*). Somewhat smaller than the Common Butterwort, this species with pale lilac flowers can be recognised by the red or purplish tinges in its leaves. It thrives in bogs and wet heaths in south-west England, a few southern counties, plentifully in the Scottish Highlands and over most of Ireland. The flowering season extends from June to October, and where the climate is mild and moist, the leafy rosettes persist through the winter. Insects are caught on the sticky leaves and it has been found that only a very few victims are required to sustain vigorous growth. Surprisingly, some greenfly attack this plant.

39 × 2·0
40 × 1·0

× 1·2

41 × 1·5
42 × 1·0

41. GREAT SUNDEW (*Drosera anglica*). Three kinds of sundew grow on our bogs and wet heaths, commonly associated with bog-mosses. Their leaves are covered with stalked, red, sticky glands which glitter in the sunshine and entrap insects which settle on them. When the victims struggle, more glands bend over to envelop them while their bodies are slowly digested. The largest is Great Sundew, with long spoon-shaped leaves, favouring the wetter parts of moors, especially in the north. Its flowers often remain closed and are self-fertilised.

42. GRASS OF PARNASSUS (*Parnassia palustris*). Although widely distributed, this species is not generally common, though it may be found in abundance locally on wet peatland. The pointed, heart-shaped leaves can be confused with those of Marsh Valerian and pass unnoticed until the startling beauty of the ivory-white, almost lily-like flowers attracts attention in late summer and autumn. As in saxifrages, the stamens bend over one by one to shed pollen on the stigmas. Small seeds are produced in great numbers in the rounded capsules.

43. CRANBERRY (*Vaccinium oxycoccus*). A slender, low-creeping plant with wiry stems and thymé-like leaves, closely related to the heathers. It is widely distributed on our wet heaths and bogs, but has been eliminated from many of its old haunts in the south by improved drainage in the last century. The attractive pink flowers appear between June and August and produce quantities of small, pear-shaped, speckled red berries. In some places these sweetish fruits are gathered in large quantities in autumn, for making jam and jelly.

43 × 1·5

44. BILBERRY (*Vaccinium myrtillus*). Also known as the whortleberry and blaeberry, this deciduous moorland shrub with green, angular twigs is common over most of Britain, excluding East Anglia and flourishes greatly in mountainous regions in the north. The bushes spread extensively by means of creeping underground shoots. The small pinkish-green flowers open in June and July. Sweet black berries, which have a grape-like bloom, ripen in autumn as the leaves turn yellow, crimson and purple.

44 × 2·0

45. CROWBERRY (*Empetrum nigrum*). A coarse, heather-like shrub which grows on both peaty and sandy soils on moors and mountains, usually in the drier places. It is to be seen mainly in Scotland, northern England, Wales and Ireland. The leaves are tightly in-curled below, with a narrow white slit showing. Small purplish-pink flowers are visible in spring and early summer, male and female developing on separate plants, and the pollen is airborne. The glossy black berries are insipid, but are eaten by many moorland birds.

46 × 1·0
47 × 2·0

46. STRAWBERRY TREE (*Arbutus unedo*). This arboreal member of the heather family is a smooth-leaved evergreen which can grow to a height of 45 ft. It abounds chiefly in countries bordering the Mediterranean, but is also a native of western Ireland, being specially plentiful on the rocky shores and islands of Killarney's famous lakes. Often growing with bilberry, heather and purple moor grass, it sometimes forms woodland with holly, durmast oak, yew and hazel. Growth is very slow and trees with trunks a yard thick can be 400 years old. The milky or pinkish flowers are at their best in October and are visited by late bees and Red Admiral butterflies. The strawberry-like fruits take slightly over a year to ripen and are edible, but rather insipid. This species is sensitive to frost.

47. DEPTFORD PINK (*Dianthus armeria*). Much resembling a miniature Sweet William, to which it is closely related, this species occurs rarely and very locally nowadays on acid, sandy or gravelly grassland and on ant-hills. It is a biennial, requiring bare soil for colonisation by the seedlings which develop in autumn and produce flowers and seeds in the following summer. The plants are often dwarfed through grazing, but can attain a height of 2 ft in favourable spots. The vivid rose-red flowers are in clusters of up to ten and have a jewel-like brilliance while open during the early part of the day, when they attract butterflies and day-flying moths. When the flowers are closed, the plants are not easy to distinguish from grass. Flowering commences in July and continues until late autumn.